Face-to-Face
PENGUINS

What's Inside?

D1371057

In an Icy World

Penguins live mainly in the far south of the world in icy oceans. They are fantastic swimmers and only visit land to have babies. Most of the time, they race through the sea! Penguins are birds, but they cannot fly. A penguin's body is covered with thick, short feathers.

African penguins are extremely noisy. Cover your ears!

Wow!
A little blue penguin only grows up to 10 inches (25 centimeters) tall. It wouldn't even reach as high as your knee!

gentoo penguin swims faster than any other penguin.

An emperor penguin is the tallest of all the penguins.

The smallest penguin is called the little blue penguin.

3

Adélie Penguin

Adélie penguins nest together in groups on the ice. Like all penguins, they have webbed feet for swimming; small, smooth heads; and long, fat bodies. Their black backs and white fronts make them look as if they are wearing suit jackets!

To walk, an Adélie penguin stands up straight and waddles along on its two short legs. It looks clumsy, but it can move faster than you!

Wait for me!

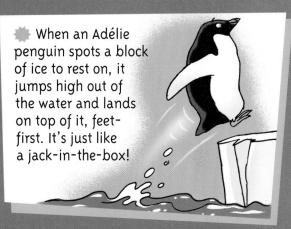

When an Adélie penguin spots a block of ice to rest on, it jumps high out of the water and lands on top of it, feet-first. It's just like a jack-in-the-box!

A male Adélie penguin is a devoted father. When a mother penguin is away at sea, he guards the babies and may not eat for up to one month!

Q How does a penguin keep warm?

A A penguin's thick feathers keep it warm. They are like a cozy blanket, trapping the heat and keeping out the bitter cold.

5

Splash and Swim!

A penguin twists, turns, and dives through the water at an incredible speed. It pushes itself along with its two stiff wings shaped like flippers. Its webbed feet and short tail help it to turn first one way, then the other.

WOW!
A penguin can hold its breath for up to 18 minutes. That's about 40 times longer than you can!

▲ Falling Over

These gentoo penguins are going for a swim. They line up on the ice, then plop headfirst into the freezing sea. They look as if they are falling in by mistake!

◢ High Jump

A penguin comes to the surface
of the water to breathe air.
It leaps in and out of the waves,
taking a deep breath each time.

Can You Believe It?

A gentoo penguin can zoom through
the water at 6 miles (10 kilometers)
per hour. That's faster than an
Olympic swimmer!

I won!

▲ Rocket Power

An emperor penguin is a champion
diver. It points its head downward,
flattens its wings against its body,
and shoots off, like an underwater
rocket, after a tasty treat.

Emperor Penguin

This tough bird is an emperor penguin. It makes its home near the icy South Pole. Here, it survives raging snowstorms and wild winds. When an emperor penguin is in a hurry, it flops onto its belly and slides along, just as if it were riding on a sled. Whoosh!

Q Why doesn't a penguin slip on the ice?

A If you tried to walk on ice, you might fall over! But a penguin doesn't. It has hooked claws at the ends of its feet that dig into the ground and give it a firm grip.

You should get a grip!

✹ An emperor penguin is a real giant. It reaches up to 4 feet (120 centimeters) in height. If you stood next to one, it would be at least as tall as you!

✹ Sometimes an emperor penguin hitches a ride on a block of ice. The wind blows its icy boat along, taking the penguin on a free ride toward the coast.

✹ During snowstorms, emperor penguins huddle together to make one big, round circle. The lucky penguins in the middle are as warm as toast!

Dinnertime

Penguins have huge appetites! These birds need to eat lots of food to stay alive in the cold weather and to get the strength to swim. A hungry penguin hunts for its dinner at sea. It feasts on juicy fish, slippery squid, and other small sea animals.

Can You Believe It?

A mother penguin swallows her food at sea, then brings it home. To feed her babies, she coughs up the food and tips the mess into their mouths!

That's delicious, Mom!

◁ **Snap It Up**

When a king penguin spots a fish, it grabs it with its hooked beak and holds it in place with its rough, spiny tongue. Then it swallows the fish whole.

WoW! Adélie penguins can swim the length of a small country to find their favorite place to eat!

▽ On the Hunt

At midnight, chinstrap penguins set off to find their dinner. They feast on hundreds of tiny creatures, called krill, that drift near the surface of the water.

◁ Danger Ahead

A penguin is a skillful hunter, but it has to watch out for larger animals ready to gobble it up. This macaroni penguin has luckily escaped from the jaws of a huge leopard seal.

Rockhopper Penguin

You can't miss a rockhopper penguin. It has a tuft of yellow and black feathers, called a crest, sticking up from its head, and a bright red beak. These little birds can live in warmer places than many other kinds of penguins. They build their nests on steep, rocky cliffs and grassy hillsides.

Q How did a rockhopper get its name?

A This penguin gets its name from the way it moves on land. Instead of walking, it hops from rock to rock. It's a real rock hopper!

It's a Laugh!
Which fish do penguins eat at night? Starfish!

Every summer, all penguins, including rockhoppers, lose their feathers. This makes the birds look really scruffy! Luckily, new feathers soon grow.

When a male rockhopper penguin meets a friendly female, he hops toward her, shakes his head, and raises his eyebrows. She's sure to be impressed!

Like all penguins, a rockhopper's black back and white front makes it difficult to spot. Hungry birds can't see it from above the waves, while seals can't spot it from below.

13

All Together Now

Each year, hundreds of thousands of penguins hop out of the icy sea to visit the land. They head up the coast like a giant army, looking for sheltered places to build their nests and have babies. The penguins all live together in a huge, noisy group called a rookery.

WOW!
Up to 600,000 penguins can live in one rookery. That's about the same as the number of people living in a large town!

◀ **Time for a Song**
A male penguin meets his mate in the rookery. To greet her, he raises his head and wings toward the sky, then sings a special tune.

Can You Believe It?

An African penguin sounds like a braying donkey! When it builds its nest, it screeches to warn other penguins to keep their distance. The noise can be heard for miles!

I can't hear myself think!

🔺It's My Patch

Even though penguins live together, they like their own space. These king penguins have all lined up facing the same way and exactly the same distance apart!

🔺 Looking for a Fight?

Rockhopper penguins pick fights, especially if they come too close to one another. They screech loudly and peck at each other with their sharp beaks.

Eggs and Nests

Most mother penguins lay two white eggs, which they place in a small nest. Both the mother and the father look after the eggs until they hatch. Some penguins build their nests with stones, while others dig burrows in the ground. A few kinds of penguins don't build nests at all.

▶ Hideaway

A little blue penguin digs a deep burrow in the sand near clumps of grass. Here, its eggs are well hidden from hungry gulls ready to snap them up.

Wow!

Penguins always return to the same place to nest. Emperor penguins march for over a week to find their homes!

◀ Take a Bow

A male Adélie penguin makes its nest from pebbles. He guards it until his mate arrives. She then gives him a deep bow to say she is ready to take over.

🔹 Fancy Footrest

A mother emperor penguin lays only one egg. She passes it to the father, who rests the egg on his feet under a flap of skin to keep it warm. The mother heads off to sea to hunt for food.

Can You Believe It?

Several penguins kept in zoos have used garbage to build their nests! They have made nests out of sticks, stones, pens, and even sunglasses.

It's a work of art!

Penguin Chick

Baby penguins are called chicks. When they hatch, they're covered in soft brown, gray, or white downy feathers. Parents look after their chicks for up to one year. During this time, the fluffy birds grow a full black-and-white feather coat.

Q How can penguins tell one another apart?

A Penguins tell one another apart by their voices. When a father penguin brings food home, he calls out. The excited chick hears and runs as fast as it can to find him.

I'm coming, Dad!

❋ Sometimes a king penguin chick overheats! Its feathers keep it so warm that on mild days, it stands in an icy stream to cool down.

❋ At first, a young gentoo penguin chick sticks close to a parent. Then, it joins a gang of other chicks in a nursery. A few grown-ups take care of the rowdy group.

❋ When food is scarce, a caring Adélie father penguin makes a special milk inside his body for his young baby to drink.

Puzzle Time

Here are a few puzzles to try. You can look back in the book to help you find the answers.

True or False?

How much do you know about penguins? Answer these true or false questions to find out.

1 Adélie penguins leap from the water and land on the ice feetfirst. Hint: Go to page 5.

2 If you stood next to an emperor penguin, it would be as tall as you. Hint: Go to page 9.

3 When a male rockhopper meets a female, he raises his foot. Hint: Go to page 13.

4 An Adélie father penguin feeds water to his baby. Hint: Go to page 19.

Whose Nest?

These three penguins are looking for their nests.
Can you help them find their way home?

Rockhopper

Little blue

Adélie

Pebble mound

Rocky burrow

Sandy burrow

Close-up

We've zoomed in on these penguins.
Can you name them?

1 Hint: Go to page 11.

2 Hint: Go to page 15.

3 Hint: Go to page 17.

Index

Created by act-two for Scholastic Inc.
Copyright © act-two, 2001.
All rights reserved. Published by Scholastic Inc.
SCHOLASTIC and associated logos are trademarks
and/or registered trademarks of Scholastic Inc.

Main illustrations: Stuart Lafford
Cartoon illustrations: All cartoon illustrations by Simon Clare
except for pp. 20-21 Geo Parkin, p. 23 Alan Rowe
Consultant: Barbara Taylor
Photographs: cover FLPA/F Lanting, pp. 4-5 Stone/Art Wolfe, pp. 8-9
Bruce Coleman Inc./Johnny Johnson, pp. 12-13 NHPA/John Shaw,
pp. 18-19 Stone/David Tipling

ISBN 0-439-31708-8

12 11 10 9 8 7 6 5 4 3   2 3 4 5 6/0

Printed in the U.S.A.

First Scholastic printing, December 2001